THE AMERICA WE LOVE

THE
AMERICA
WE
LOVE

LARAINE DAY

DOWNE PUBLISHING, INCORPORATED

CONTENTS

"Let us tell all Americans that we should love America. But let us love her not because she is strong, but because America is a good country and we are going to make her better."
RICHARD M. NIXON, JUNE 25, 1970

INTRODUCTION

Never underestimate the power of one person, one people, one nation.

As I travel across the country for the National Association of Real Estate Boards, in support of their "Make America Better" campaign, I learn more and more about the inner feelings of Americans. And I sense that we are seeking some kind of participation, a new communal purpose.

Just as our nation has advanced from frontier to frontier for almost 200 years, so it can find greatness again—from the heart and soul of its people. And we are a people willing to believe in our country, willing to work to convert a perplexing period of change into an opportunity for service.

Because your spirit has lifted mine, I decided to write this book. With the collaboration of Lenore Hershey, of the *Ladies' Home Journal*, I have assembled thoughts great and small, personal and borrowed observations, into a love letter to America.

Whatever your age, your beliefs or your politics, I hope my book inspires you to think more about the positive values of our beloved country...as well as about how to heal its wounds and solve its problems.

LARAINE DAY

1
LOOKING BACKWARD THE HERITAGE

"For I believe that out of the whole body of our past, out of our differences, our quarrels, our many interests and directions, something has emerged that is itself unique in the world: America—complicated, paradoxical, bullheaded, shy, cruel, boisterous, unspeakably dear, and very beautiful."

JOHN STEINBECK

HOMEWORK

"What is history?" I once asked my daughter, and she answered, "Homework." Our children, encouraged to live in a perpetual present, should be given a better view of American history, one that is more than a textbook, a dry-as-dust lecture or a mossy myth that the young are too sophisticated to believe. Perhaps it is time to bring American history home, to make it part of breakfast and dinner table conversation. To read it aloud together. To use it as the central theme of that next visit to Plymouth Rock, or tour of Civil War battlefields. To incorporate it into our lives through American arts and crafts, through our poets and our music-makers, through our recognition of the many regional cultures that feed into the mainstream of life in these United States. And, above all, to make American history real by being able to answer our children's questions. That may mean some homework for *us*. But it will be worth the effort for us all to discover and rediscover aspects of our heritage.

"There is little that is more important
for an American citizen to know than
the history and traditions of his country.
Without such knowledge, he stands
uncertain and defenseless before the
world, knowing neither where he
has come from, nor where he is going."
JOHN F. KENNEDY

"Dig history," I heard a bearded young teacher telling his class. "It's over thirty, but it's full of cool characters and relevant scenarios. And if you're going to rebel against the Establishment, get into the way it was established."

"Being thus arrived in a good harbor and brought safe to land, they fell on their knees and blessed the God of Heaven who had brought them over the vast and furious ocean and delivered them from all the perils and miseries thereof."

WILLIAM BRADFORD (HISTORY OF PLYMOUTH PLANTATION)

ONE NATION INDIVISIBLE

Our "one nation indivisible" has always known the threat of division. Even the sage of Philadelphia, Benjamin Franklin, admitted in 1787 that the U.S. Constitution he endorsed might have faults. His reasoning:

"When you assemble a number of men, to have their joint wisdom, you inevitably assemble with those men all their prejudices, their passions, their errors of opinion, their local interests and their selfish views. From such an assembly can a perfect production be expected?"

If the Founding Fathers had their differences, Franklin was a mending man. He went on to urge the delegates to the Constitutional Convention to forget their disagreements and unanimously agree on the text of a Constitution. He said:

> *"Much of the strength and efficiency of any government, in procuring and securing happiness to the people, depends on opinion, and the general opinion of the goodness of the government as well as the wisdom and integrity of its governors."*

There is criticism for improvement's sake, and criticism just for criticism's sake. Once, when Winston Churchill was building a brick wall, he was annoyed by a fault-finder. Told that the wall was crooked, Churchill said, "Any fool can see what's wrong. But can you see what's right?"

> *"Let not him who is houseless pull down the house of another: but let him labor diligently and build one for himself, thus by example assuring that his own shall be safe from violence when built."*
>
> ABRAHAM LINCOLN

Black studies are valuable, because all peoples should have a prideful knowledge of their origins and racial achievements. Our history shows how all colors, creeds and races helped to build this country...and must work together for our future. A review of history shows that every Presidential election year is filled with heated rhetoric. But Abraham Lincoln had a calming bit of wisdom on that subject which applies at all times:

*"While the people retain their virtue
and vigilance, no administration, by
any extreme of wickedness or folly,
can seriously injure the government in the short space of four years."*

NEEDLING

As early as 1650, young girls were embroidering samplers, and there still exists a piece of embroidery worked by the daughter of Miles Standish. When George Washington died in 1799, many women and girls embroidered memorial pictures and verses. Patty Polk, of Kent, Maryland, who was ten years old that year, depicted on canvas a tombstone marked with the initials "GW." But she left a legacy of obstinate honesty to remind us that little girls don't change much. On the bottom of her work she embroidered:

*"Patty Polk did this and she
hated every stitch she did in it.
She loves to read much more."*

5

UTOPIANS

Dropouts and copouts are nothing new. America in the nineteenth century had scores of communes like Brook Farm in New England, and New Harmony in Indiana. One who tried the "simple living and high thinking" at Brook Farm was Nathaniel Hawthorne. He left after six months.

At the age of twenty-seven Henry David Thoreau built a cabin on the bank of Walden Pond, where he lived alone for two years and wrote his famous book about nature, "Walden."

Thoreau was a loner, seemingly not interested in activism. Ralph Waldo Emerson, his close friend, thought he was wasting his talents, once protesting that "instead of engineering for all America," Thoreau was "the captain of a huckleberry party." Thoreau did take stands though. Throughout his writings he protested the destruction of wildlife and the countryside. And he went to jail rather than pay a tax to the government that defended Negro slavery. While he was in jail, so the story goes, he was visited by Emerson. "Why are you in there?" Emerson shouted through the bars. "Why are you out there?" retorted Thoreau.

> *"I have sworn upon the altar of God,*
> *eternal hostility against every form*
> *of tyranny over the mind of man."*
> THOMAS JEFFERSON

Loners and joiners; dreamers and doers. The history of America encompasses every kind of hero: warriors, visionaries, innovators, industrialists, gallant fools, majestic madmen, ruffians and intellectuals, clowns and prophets. Today, some of our young people are turning to other heroes. Often these young rebels dismiss much of the hard work and success of America as mere materialism.

Because we cannot bring peace to the world in a night or wipe out poverty in a day, our good qualities as Americans are sometimes lost to view. Youthful impatience is forgivable; indeed, it is part of the American tradition. The values that sincere young idealists cherish—social, moral, educational and political—are all there to be seen in the record of our country, in the goals set by our best leaders, in a system that sometimes falters in its fine intentions but largely fulfills them.

Or in the words of Adlai E. Stevenson:

"When an American says he loves his country,
he means not only that he loves the New
England hills, the prairies glistening in the
sun, the wide and rising plains, the
great mountains and the sea. He means that he
loves an inner air, an inner light in which
freedom lives, and in which a man can draw the
breath of self-respect."

2
LOOKING FORWARD
THE PROMISE

"Man has already transformed nature; are we to say he is unable to transform himself? Is it reasonable to believe that a species that has demonstrated a capacity to lift itself off the planet is unable to raise its sights in devising a rational future? If awareness of the consequences of the present drift leads to a desire to avert them, the Age of Acceleration can lead to an Age of Balance."

NORMAN COUSINS

INVOLVEMENT

"I never think of the future. It comes soon enough," said Einstein. But now it's as fashionable to paint America's future black as it is to wear long hair, love beads, and suede boots. If we don't end in chaos and revolution, we'll be poisoned by pollution. Our children's grandchildren won't have standing room and they'll have computerized numbers, not names. That is, if we're not all charred to cinders when somebody pushes the wrong button.

Doom, gloom and futility. The whole world at a dead end, strangled in its own complexity. God is gone, faith is outdated. The United States? You know who's ruining the country. (Fill in the name of your favorite scapegoat group.)

But have you detected recently a tiny change — an upbeat? Encouraging evidence of adjustment, accommodation? A new recognition that order, instead of disorder, *could* bring needed social changes? There's the sound of a new marching music, one that could help get our country back on its tracks. It's a rejection of helplessness. It's called involvement.

"The best way out is always through."
ROBERT FROST

It's also called *action*. And there's action everywhere. Women ask, "How can I help? What can I do?" The involved woman is the truly liberated woman. Young people are moving from political extremism toward the center, realizing that pursuit of the most shining ideals must start from a secure base. Businessmen are recognizing that what's good for the community and the country is good for business. The ones I know best, the Realtors of America, have started a program called "Make America Better." The projects vary. A mini-park in a ghetto area of San Antonio, Texas; drug abuse programs in other Texas cities. A clubhouse for black youths in Des Moines, Iowa. A mental health complex in Bellingham, Washington. An educational program on open housing in Indianapolis, Indiana. A "Light the Night" campaign to discourage crime in scores of cities and towns. In each case, hundreds of citizens were involved.

> *"All this will not be finished in the first 100 days. Nor will it be finished in the first 1,000 days, nor in the life of this Administration, nor even perhaps in our lifetime on this planet. But let us begin."*
> JOHN F. KENNEDY,
> INAUGURAL ADDRESS, JANUARY 20, 1961

3
OUR LAND

"I think in all the world the like abundance is not to be found."
SIR WALTER RALEIGH'S AGENT, VIRGINIA, 1584

AMERICA AND ECOLOGY

Today our national abundance is threatened by our shortsighted mistakes in tampering with nature, so we are concerned with ecology—from the Greek *oikos*, a house, meaning literally the science that deals with the home conditions of living organisms. Man's house, the world, is being polluted and eroded. The ecologists are working to restore nature's delicate balance, and conservationists are fighting for nature's beauty with contemporary battle tactics. In their zeal, some of them tend to condemn any industrial expansion as a sort of conspiracy. On the other side, many corporations and government agencies shut their eyes to the long-range effects of the steps they take.

If we love America—and life—we can no longer ignore or justify pollution of our air and water, or wanton destruction of our fields and forests. Just talking about environment is not enough. It is a question of replacing selfishness with a new awareness of our shared crisis.

THE OASES

Meanwhile, there are the oases—the places reserved and preserved; pockets of quietude in the maze of super-highways and megalopolises.

More than 200 areas are administered by the National Park Services. Like Everglades and Sequoia, and Acadia in Maine, and the whole Cape Cod National Seashore with its 40-mile coastline.

Like Grand Teton in Wyoming, where elk and moose roam, and the rare trumpeter swan swims in the lakes. Like the Grand Canyon and Bryce National Park in Utah, where outsized rock gardens soar skyward more than seven thousand feet above sea level. We've had these nature preserves since 1864, when Congress set aside the majestic Yosemite Valley as a park to be "inalienable for all time," a memorial to our once mighty wildernesses.

> *"Climb the mountains and get their good tidings. Nature's peace will flow into you as the sunshine flows into trees."*
> JOHN MUIR, WHO IN 1892 HELPED FOUND THE SIERRA CLUB

"The Age of Ecology has hit us," writes a friend from Pennsylvania. "Our 12-year-old Diane wants a bird-feeder for her birthday, and 14-year-old Ralph insists on washing his football uniforms with old-fashioned laundry soap and soda. Sixteen-year-old Eric, his stereo blasting away, is writing a paper on noise pollution. I've promised the kids I'll have pesticide night at the garden club if *they* promise to keep their rooms neater."

> *"I like trees because they seem more resigned to the way they have to live than other things do."*
> WILLA CATHER

A Florida landscape architect, who said he preferred beautification to pollution, decided to hand out plants instead of cigars on the birth of his first child.

Early Americans valued trees as standing timber to be sawed up for houses, tables and axe handles, and much of our early economy was based on lumbering. Since then, we have spent some 200 years using up our timberland. Today, however, our forests begin to prosper, thanks to conservation programs. And there are almost 800 million acres of woodlands in America, and almost 900 species of trees.

But trees are needed in our own backyards. Here are 10 kinds of trees which have varieties that thrive in most parts of the country: oak, crabapple, hawthorn, pine, ginkgo, flowering dogwood (not in very cold areas), maple, holly, honey locust and ash. How about planting a few yourself?

"A nation's history is written in the book of its word, the book of its art. A people's history is also written in what they do with the natural beauty Providence bestowed upon them."
RICHARD M. NIXON, FEBRUARY 8, 1971

YOU CAN GO HOME

The miracle of modern jet plane travel has turned our vast land into a one-day excursion. The white jet contrails tie us all together in the sky. And below, on a clear day, all our grandeurs are set out before us: the checkerboard farms, the snow-topped peaks, the soft green mountains, the endless plains, the sudden cities.

Most of all, I enjoy landing in a city just after twilight. I look down (even through smog) with awe and enchantment into the fairy embroidery of distant lights. Behind those lighted windows are thousands of loving dinners cooking on the range. And there are red-tailed, ant-sized cars threading homeward on the skeins of highways.

Could Columbus have believed it? Could our Founding Fathers have dreamed of it? Does anyone down there know how beautiful, how welcoming, it all looks from here? Are we not all indeed blessed to be part of it, to go home every evening in the free United States of America?

> "The dawn Rides the low east...
> First are the capes, then are the
> shorelands, now The blue Appalachians
> ...The willows shudder with light
> on the long Ohio: The Lakes scatter
> the low sun: the prairies Slide out
> of the dark...up from the high
> plains of Wyoming: The steep Sierras
> arise: the struck foam Flames at
> the wind's heel on the far Pacific."
> ARCHIBALD MACLEISH

4

OUR PEOPLES

"It's a complex fate, being an American."
HENRY JAMES

"Join the United States and join the family."
ROBERT FROST

WHAT ARE AMERICANS?

Americans are 204 million people who come in every size, shape and color. You are probably talking to an American when you ask for the name of the President of the United States and get the correct answer, followed by "And in my opinion, he's...." In America, if you've got an opinion, you state it. Some Americans still affirm, "My country, right or wrong." But many others say, "My country, but not extreme right or left."

A really subversive idea is to want all of us to look, think, and act the same way. It would deny the whole point of America...a country dedicated to finding unity in diversity.

> *"These states are the amplest*
> *poem, Here is not merely a nation,*
> *but a teeming Nation of nations."*
> WALT WHITMAN

As to a magnet, our ancestors came. They were the world's restless and dispossessed looking for something better. White, yellow, brown people; and the black people who, unlike the others, in the beginning were forced to come. First the Norsemen, then an Italian sailing on behalf of Spain. Then Portuguese, English, French. Then successive waves of other peoples: Irish, Germans, Russians, Scot, Chinese and Japanese, Jew, Greek, Italian, Scandinavian. Most recently, Mexican and Puerto Rican.

They came for a variety of reasons. But with grit, hard work, and a little bit of luck, they made a new life in a new world. Except for the Indians, we are all descended from immigrants who left us many heritages, including a talent for moving from the bottom of society toward the top. It is this possibility which makes America unique.

> *"I believe freedom comes the hard way—by ceaseless groping, toil, struggle— even by fiery trial and agony."*
> CARL SANDBURG

SKINS OF RED, SKINS OF BROWN

I was born on a Ute reservation in Utah, where my father was a translator for the Indians. My brother and I are twins, and one of my early memories is of tribesmen standing in our front yard, watching curiously, because twins are rare among Indians.

We must pay more attention to the plight of the Indians. It was no act of generosity that prompted the Pilgrim Fathers to invite Chief Massasoit and ninety of his braves to share the first Thanksgiving feast. It was a debt of gratitude which has never been fully repaid.

My husband serves on the board of the Polynesian Cultural Center in Laie, Hawaii, forty miles north of Honolulu. "We in Hawaii have a tendency to forget that our state is also one of the great Polynesian nations," he says. He is working to preserve another culture that is part of our Pacific heritage. Skins of red, skins of brown. These groups were *original* Americans.

> *"I am the inferior of any man whose rights I trample under foot. Men are not superior by reason of the accidents of race or color. They are superior who have the best heart—the best brain."*
> ROBERT GREEN INGERSOLL

FOODS: QUALITY AND QUANTITY

Did you ever realize how many of our favorite dishes are American Indian in origin? Corn, of course. But also barbeque, and spoon bread. And cranberry sauce, mincemeat pie, even baked clams, and so-called Boston baked beans.

Our tables are an ethnic combination. But there are some foods as American as apple pie. Like apple pie. And shoofly pie. And cheese from our rich dairylands, and hot dogs on rolls, and peanuts and popcorn, and ice cream in countless flavors, and flapjacks with maple syrup. The menu is end-less. The ordinary supermarket in the United States today carries more than 7,000 items.

Even if the future promises us gourmet meals of spun soybean fiber, the American palate will not suffer. Eating well, with gusto, is part of our recipe for keeping vital.

When they learn of the need, Americans cannot

endure the idea of anyone going hungry. We are not a "let-them-eat-cake" people. We are a school-lunch-for-every-child, food-stamps-for-the-deprived kind of people. That, too, is part of the American recipe for keeping vital.

AND ALL RELIGIONS

The First Amendment grants Americans the right to worship in their own way. God is still alive and well in the United States. You can even see His hand extended to all those who worship these days with rock masses, switched-on Scriptures and other efforts to make religion more "relevant."

> *"The real faith of America is decided*
> *between ten and eleven in the morning*
> *when the women gather for a second cup of*
> *coffee. It is their discussion,*
> *their give-and-take, which affects the total*
> *community. If the minister rocks the boat*
> *on Sunday, his ideas are digested*
> *in these morning seminars—and passed along*
> *on the most personal basis to the family."*
> DR. KRISTER STENDAHL,
> *DEAN OF THE HARVARD DIVINITY SCHOOL*

MY FAITH

I belong to a denomination that was created in America: The Church of Jesus Christ of the Latter Day Saints, which makes me a Mormon. In the last 20 years, membership in our church has doubled to almost three million. That's a long way from the 1840's, when, to escape persecution and to find a safe home, 80,000 Mormon pioneers, led by Brigham Young, crossed thousands of miles of mountains and plains to reach the valley of the Great Salt Lake. Some walked, some rode, and more than 6,000 died on this cross-country pilgrimage. The Mormons believe that a war was fought in heaven for freedom. That's one reason why they think this free land is so worth believing in.

THE AMERICAN WOMAN

In 1920 the Nineteenth Amendment to the Constitution was ratified granting women the right to vote. But the women's rights movement goes on.

> *"We would have every arbitrary barrier thrown down. We would have every path laid open to Woman as freely as to Man. Were this done, and a slight temporary fermentation allowed to subside, we should see crystallizations more pure and of more various beauty."*
> MARGARET FULLER, 1845

AMERICANS ARE

Family people. Even though social habits are changing, 87% of Americans still live and thrive in the old-fashioned two-parent family unit.

Inventive people: Franklin, Whitney, Colt, Edison, Burbank, Carver...the names of American inventors are part of our legend. American inventions range from the airplane and the adding machine to the typewriter, vacuum cleaner and zipper.

"For half a century, we called on unbounded invention and untiring industry to create an order of plenty for all our people. The challenge of the next half century is whether we have the wisdom to use that wealth to enrich and elevate our national life—and to advance the quality of American civilization."
LYNDON B. JOHNSON, 1964

WHERE THE PEOPLE ARE

Our six most populated cities are New York, Chicago, Los Angeles, Philadelphia, Detroit and Houston, in that order. But do you know the three fastest-growing counties? They are Mohave, Arizona; Vernon, Louisiana, and Pitkin, Colorado. Keep your eye on these: they're the frontiers of tomorrow.

"I came from a state that raises corn and cotton and cocklebur and Democrats, and frothy eloquence neither convinces nor satisfies me. I am from Missouri. You have got to show me."
WILLARD DUNCAN VANDIVER, 1899

5
OUR HOMES

"Peace be to this house."
A CURRIER AND IVES MOTTO, 1872

NOSTALGIA

Nostalgia literally means homesickness, a yearning for that piece of the past which seemed warmer, simpler, a time-veiled haven. Isn't that why we reach for old-fashioned cooking, baking bread, needlework and patchwork? And the memories of porches, whatnot cabinets, country kitchens, root cellars are so appealing?

Americans are home-lovers, even in the seventies. With our modern conveniences, appliances, with carports and swimming pools, with changing life styles, we still want a center for our most significant human contacts, a place of grace and comfort, a home.

In my own house I am king. (Spanish) Our own home surpasses every other. (Latin)

> *"Mid pleasures and places though we may roam, Be it ever so humble, there's no place like home; A charm from the skies seems to hallow us there, Which sought through the world is ne'er met with elsewhere."*
>
> *JOHN HOWARD PAYNE*

THE OLD THINGS

Antique America is a big thing today. Old snuff boxes, shaving mugs, bottles, walking sticks, powder flasks, cookie molds...all manner of commonplace objects of another day bring high prices. According to the Parke-Bernet Galleries in New

York, a Philadelphia Chippendale chair will fetch ten times what an English Chippendale would, just because it's American. Who knows—our great-grandchildren may collect tape recorders and electric toothbrushes. And ask their parents wistfully, "What was an attic? What was a front porch?"

> *"To us, our house was not an*
> *unsentient matter—it had a heart*
> *and soul, and eyes to see us with; and*
> *approvals, and solicitudes, and deep*
> *sympathies; it was of us, and we were*
> *in its confidence, and lived in its grace*
> *and in the peace of its benediction.*
> *We never came home from an absence that*
> *its face did not light up and speak*
> *out its eloquent welcome—and we could*
> *not enter it unmoved."*
>
> MARK TWAIN

HOUSE TOUR

Some day I would like to take a house tour through this entire nation. Mount Vernon...Monticello... Brigham Young's Beehive House, echoing the mansions of his native Vermont...the Abraham Lincoln home in Springfield, Illinois...Helen Keller's birthplace in Tuscumbia, Alabama...Leland Stanford's house in Sacramento, California...the house in Boston where John F. Kennedy was born...the antebellum mansions that still exist near Natchez, Mississippi...So many different styles, so many different homes that nurtured so many of our great Americans. Everyone, of course, should visit the White House in Washington, D.C. Here, under one roof, is history, style, and continuity.

"I pray Heaven to bestow the best of blessings on this house, and all that shall hereafter inhabit it. May none but honest and wise men ever rule under this roof."

JOHN ADAMS, 1800
(WHITE HOUSE BLESSING, ENGRAVED ON
FIREPLACE IN STATE DINING ROOM BY
DIRECTION OF FRANKLIN D. ROOSEVELT)

MODERN HOUSEKEEPING

Your grandmother probably had allotted tasks for every day of the week: Monday, washing; Tuesday, ironing; Wednesday, mending; Thursday, shopping; Friday, cleaning; Saturday, baking; Sunday, church-going. Today, with all our appliances working for us ...ranges, washers and dryers, vacuum cleaners, garbage disposers and all the rest...schedules are no longer rigid. Yet two recent surveys reveal that we haven't changed all *that* much. According to a study made by W. J. Hagerty & Sons, Ltd., the average suburban homemaker spends 19.8 hours a week cleaning her house, while the city homemaker spends even more—32 hours a week. And a 1970 poll by Louis

Harris of a broad span of American women asked what they found most enjoyable about being a woman today. "Being a mother, raising a family, being a homemaker" outranked everything else.

THE FRAGRANCE OF HOME

A house always has a special fragrance. A clean home *smells* clean. In some friends' homes, you can close your eyes and know where you are because of interesting aromas from the kitchen, a pleasant whiff of lavender from the closet. You can create house fragrances with pine pillows from Maine, aromatic woods for your fireplace, flower potpourris, bayberry and other scented candles. And, if you're lazy, there are always the aerosol sprays!

BEAUTIFICATION AND RESTORATION

Mrs. Albert D. Lasker is a great lady who loves flowers so much that she donates huge plantings to a number of cities. Mrs. Lasker feels that we should all raise our own flowers. "Take any new house, or an old house," she says."Imagine the yard with blossoming trees, roses on the fence, borders of tulips and daffodils on the path to the front door. We can each make our homes and towns more beautiful."

All over our nation, people are realizing that we cannot let the past disappear in our rush to the future. Citizens with a sense of beauty and history are joining together to preserve landmark buildings, historic neighborhoods with a unique texture

31

and flavor. San Francisco, Philadelphia, Denver, Providence, New Orleans, Richmond are restoring and preserving selected homes and areas. And the National Historic Preservation Act has made it possible to protect one of our great natural resources: our past.

Restorations and museums of Americana abound, such as Williamsburg, the colonial capital of Virginia: eighteenth century living at its most gracious. The Henry Ford Museum and Greenfield Village, Dearborn, Michigan, is an indoor-outdoor museum reflecting almost every phase of American history. The Henry Francis DuPont Museum, Winterthur, Delaware, houses the largest collection of American furniture and decorative arts in the country, covering two hundred years from 1640 to 1840. The Polynesian Cultural Center is in Laie, Oahu, Hawaii. There is Old Sturbridge Village in Mass.; the restored homes of Newport, R.I.; Monticello, Jefferson's home at Charlottesville, Va.; Independence National Historic Park in Philadelphia; the gold-rush mining camps at Columbia, Sutter's Creek, and Angel's Camp, California; and many, many others.

BUT WHAT ABOUT THE PRESENT?

In *American Home* magazine, Senator Edmund Muskie had some interesting things to say about young people today. He wrote, "They want a place to let down their guard; to strengthen relationships; to stretch their minds." Then he added, significantly,

"The young people of our diverse society read new meaning into the old cliche, 'Be it ever so humble, there's no place like home'. They are sensitive to the fact that too many Americans live in substandard homes that rob them of the dignity which is their birthright. We cannot consider the home as an institution relevant to this century until every man has a decent house."

What makes a new house a good house? Quality and lastingness. What makes a neighborhood a good neighborhood? Quality and lastingness, but conscience, too. The National Opinion Research Center found that stable, racially integrated neighborhoods are not rare at all. It is estimated that 36 million Americans, in 11 million households, live in integrated neighborhoods, or about one American in every five.

GOOD NEIGHBORS

When the first New England settlers arrived, and built the houses they called "salt boxes," after colonial salt containers, they would have a "raising bee." The whole community would gather to "raise" the house in a great collective effort. "Raising bees" are still possible. We can join together to improve our streets, our communities, our cities, our nation. We can learn to subdue our fears and strengthen our understandings—as neighbors we must. We can foster love and principle and courage.

That's what truly makes a house a home!

6

OUR TRADITIONS

"We must act and build out of our own spirits. How? How? We continually need new politics, new cities, new marriages and families, new ways of work and leisure. We also need the fine old ways."

HERBERT GOLD

OUR TRADITIONS

American traditions encompass everything from rallying cries ("Go West, young man") to Fourth of July fireworks. The dictionary defines tradition as any belief, custom or way of life which has its roots in one's family, or racial or national past; a long-established convention.

There is nothing conventional about the American mythical heroes. Some, like Davy Crockett, or John Henry and Casey Jones, the railroad men, were real men metamorphosed into myths. Others, like Paul Bunyan (and his Blue Ox Babe), belong to our tradition of making up tall stories.

Traditions may change: some will fall by the wayside, others will persist. But the best traditions provide a framework for our daily experience.

HOLIDAYS

The history of American Christmas celebrations really began in 1492, when Columbus ran aground on a reef and was wrecked off the island of Hispaniola on Christmas Eve. He and his crew were saved by the Indians, and the following day he feasted with their chief. Later, he built a fortress nearby and named it La Navidad, or the Nativity.

While Christmas is celebrated in many countries of the world, America has a number of its own holidays and traditions associated with them. We have Arbor Day (April 22) when children plant trees, and Labor Day, the end-of-summer celebration, in honor of the working man. But we also have Seward's Day (March 30, Alaska); Kamehameha Day (June 11, Hawaii); Defender's Day (September 12, Maryland); Mecklinburg Day (May 20, North Carolina); Cherokee Strip Day (September 16, Oklahoma); Pioneer Day (July 24, Utah); and Town Meeting Day (March 3, Vermont). Each has a special meaning.

Thanksgiving Day is uniquely American — a time when the whole nation gathers for the traditional turkey feast. Families rejoin, and fourteen people of all ages at the dinner table is the rule rather than the exception. Thanksgiving is itself — a time of giving thanks for our many joys; our homes, our families, our communities, and our nation.

OLD GLORY

June 14 is Flag Day, the day we honor the "stars and stripes." Traditionally, George Washington designed the first American flag, which Betsy Ross sewed in 1776. The flag has been important to us always. In 1814, Francis Scott Key described it in a poem which was set to music and became our national anthem.

"And the star-spangled banner in triumph shall wave, O'er the land of the free and the home of the brave."

One of the tragedies of our time is the way our flag has become a rope in a tug-of-war. But its old meaning endures. Hearts beat faster when Neil Armstrong planted a wire-stiffened Old Glory on the moon. Whether the flag appears on the seat of the pants of a defiant youngster or at the head of a parade, it is yet a symbol and one does not fight or die for a piece of cloth, but for a total country.

THE AMERICAN EAGLE

The Federal Eagle's origins date back to the ancient phoenix, the legendary bird of immortality. To the American Indian, the eagle signified wisdom. But the eagle has not always been our national symbol. In fact, it took six years of talk and three committees (another American tradition) before Congress in 1782 approved the present design of the Great Seal. Benjamin Franklin thought that the wild turkey should be the national bird! President Harry S. Truman reminded us after World War II, when the nations of the world were struggling to evolve the United Nations to prevent further such wars, that the Federal Eagle faces the sheaths of peace rather than the arrows of war in our Great Seal.

UNCLE SAM

Samuel Wilson was a genial, upright gentleman who shipped large quantities of meat to our soldiers in the War of 1812. The soldiers called the food "Uncle Sam's beef" and use of the name gradually widened to designate as "Uncle Sam's" all property belonging to the U.S. Government.

Uncle Sam is still a popular symbol for government from the cartoonist's satiric pen to the traditional poster saying that "Uncle Sam Wants You!"

POLITICS

There are many American traditions associated with politics but particularly in a national election campaign. The way it appears in the newspapers, the winning candidate is the one who wears the biggest ten-gallon hat, eats the widest variety of ethnic foods, and kisses the most babies.

> *"Paul Douglas says that milking
> cows on his step-parents' farm
> in Maine was fine training for a
> politician's handshake; 'the
> hand movement is about the same.'"*
> T. R. B. *(THE NEW REPUBLIC)*

For all the foolery of an election campaign, the issues are debated, from Lincoln and Douglas in the 1860's to Nixon and Kennedy in the 1960's. And although Richard Nixon was said to have "lost" the television debates, he went on to win the Presidency eight years later. That, too, is in the American tradition of democracy at work.

BASEBALL

Sports are one of America's greatest traditions. Since I was once married to Leo Durocher, I got to know a lot about baseball, and about the wonderful men who played the game. Willie Mays...Alvin Dark...Sal Maglie...Bobby Thomson from the Giant team. Pee Wee Reese and Ralph Branca from the Dodgers. Phil Rizzuto of the Yankees, whom they once wouldn't allow into the Stork Club because they didn't recognize him out of uniform.

> *"Take off the goat-horns, Dodgers,*
> *that egret which two very fine*
> *base-stealers can offset. You've got*
> *plenty: Jackie Robinson and Campy and*
> *big Newk, and Dodgerdom again*
> *watching everything you do. You won*
> *last year. Come on."*
> MARIANNE MOORE

Americans are great team-rooters. I'm afraid I broke with tradition there. I'd get so loyal to the men that when they were traded, I couldn't bear to root against them.

MOVIES

Movies really began in America. Think of the silent "flicks" which had printed dialogue and were accompanied by piano players musically capturing each mood! D. W. Griffith's *Birth of a Nation* was a milestone in cinema history. And the talent — Charlie Chaplin, the Gishes, Harold Lloyd, Buster Keaton, Mary Pickford and Douglas Fairbanks.

As a former movie star myself, I sometimes think that today's films leave us feeling unmoved, degraded or confused. Audiences, however, are consumers and can help shape the product by support or rejection at the box office. That's part of the American tradition, too.

SO MANY SPECIAL RICHES

There are so many other things that are part of our way of life. Square dancing...country fairs...the circus coming to town...Valentine's Day...azalea, apple blossom, and lilac festivals, not to mention the Tournament of Roses in Pasadena...Hallowe'en ...popular music from "country and Western" to rock and roll...carpools and potluck suppers... Masons, Shriners, Elks, Lions and all the other fraternal, social and service groups that combine sociable and social aims...rodeos and salmon fishing derbies...Bowl games, boat races...Boy Scouts, Girl Scouts, and 4-H Clubs...January sales...April Fool's Day...and those quaint epitaphs that can be found on the tombstones in New England cemeteries. Like the one in Lincoln, Maine, which reads:

"1800: Sacred to the Memory of Jared Bates.
His widow, aged 24, living at 7 Elm Street
has every qualification for a good wife
and yearns to be comforted."

Waste not, want not; another American tradition!

7

OUR HOPES

"Ah! What would the world be to us
If the children were no more?
We should dread the desert behind us
Worse than the dark before."
HENRY WADSWORTH LONGFELLOW

OUR CHILDREN ARE OUR HOPES

If, to feed the world, we must limit our population and plan our families, we can do it. But let us not lose our awe for the greatest act of creation: the high point of love which is the miracle of a wanted child. If we can't have our own children, or choose not to, let us open our homes and hearts to the ones who need us. As the mother of four — two by natural birth, two adopted — I know that, as Swinburne put it, "Where children are not, heaven is not."

One father said to another, "I have nothing against young people. I just hope my kid doesn't become one." Our children are our hopes. Let us tame our fears for their future, and see each other, young and old, as human beings.

EDUCATION

We've come a long way from the simplicity of the little red schoolhouse in America. The number of young adults with college degrees has almost tripled since 1940, and 75% of our young people have completed high school. The subject of education, of every level from nursery school to graduate school, is endlessly discussed. Some people feel we worry too much about our young people's schooling, but education is the highest expression of American ideals and attitudes. And the system must always be open to critical view...and to improvement. Education, too, provides hope. It enriches our lives, and is a key to the future.

An educated population is an enlightened one. Even our form of government, which requires the participation of everyone to be sustained or improved, can only benefit from an educated citizenry.

> *"Democracy has to be born anew*
> *every generation."*
> JOHN DEWEY

It is the young who are often our idealists, our innovators. Their demands for the quick solution, the immediate end to the obvious problem are oversimplified; their frustration at inaction can take extreme forms. But the flow of American life depends on them, too. They are our hopes.

> *"What we must do first of all is listen.*
> *Young people are trying to tell us*
> *something. They are probably right in*
> *much of what they say, however wrong*
> *their prescriptions for righting matters.*
> *Then we must respond."*
> DANIEL P. MOYNIHAN

DAUGHTERESE

"I'm getting dressed." (She's in the bathtub.) "I'm almost dressed." (She's putting on her panty-hose.) "I'm dressed." (She's in the closet, looking for the skirt that's at the cleaners.) Randy's *gross.*" (He didn't notice her.) "Randy's OK." (He said hello today.) "Randy? Randy who?" (He definitely noticed her.) "May I use the phone for one short call?" (Her best friend has to hear.) "I only talked five minutes!" (Thirty-five.) "They're not my kind of kids; too fast." (She's really been listening to us.) "I love you, Mom. I love you, Dad." (We've really been listening to her.)

> *"Oh, what a tangled web*
> *do parents weave*
> *When they think that their*
> *children are naive."*
> OGDEN NASH

WEDDINGS

The college prom has faded, and iconoclastic youth seeks changes in the traditional wedding ceremony. Indeed, a loosening of morals and a new sexual freedom seem to be challenging the very institution of marriage itself.

Father Michael Gallagher of St. Patrick's Cathedral in New York has said, "I have met some young people who have tried this living together thing... The question in their minds during the living together period was, 'Do you love me enough so that you are willing to stand up in front of other people and *say* that you love me?'"

When young people want changes in the wedding ceremony, they are often asking for reflection, a search for communion in relationships. These changes can be meaningful to us all, and are often age-old in their wisdom—excerpts from the *Koran* or the Indian sages. And contemporary—folk songs of special meaning and relevance, poetry, philosophical writings. The *Bible* is not neglected—*Psalms*, the *Song of Solomon*, *Proverbs*, *Deuteronomy*. The changes can be significant—to the ceremony, to the public event, to the meaningfulness of a marriage.

OUR CHILDREN

Children have a special place in this country's culture, partly because we are a young-minded nation, and partly because we are a loving nation. Many children in deprived countries around the world are born with small chance of living to maturity. Most American children are well-nourished, sheltered, cared-for, and can expect to live to the Biblical three-score-and-ten. While some of fortune's most chosen children have turned their backs on comfort, some of the neglected are asking for a chance to enjoy it. We must cherish *all* our children, for they are our hopes.

> *"I happen, temporarily, to occupy this*
> *White House. I am living witness*
> *that any one of your children may*
> *look to come here as my father's child has."*
> ABRAHAM LINCOLN

8

OUR RESPONSIBILITIES

*"Observe good faith and justice
toward all nations.
Cultivate peace and harmony with all."*
GEORGE WASHINGTON

THE VALUE OF BEING AN AMERICAN

We hear a lot about rights today, but very little about responsibilities, probably because it's more pleasant to think about belonging to the club than about paying dues. I happen to believe that being an American is the best bargain in nationality in the world, which is why I bite my tongue when I'm tempted, as everyone is, to grumble about paying taxes. Taxes are the dues we pay for belonging to the club, for having all the things we take for granted, from city streets to parks, expressways, moon walks, medical advances, our agricultural research, our judicial system, our national defense, and of course, our education. We may have our own ideas on how our tax money should be apportioned; nevertheless it boils down to this: For the best in available nations, for our energized democracy with its lifetime guarantee, taxes are a small price to pay. Whatever we give to the Internal Revenue Service, we get a bargain.

SERVICE

There's a lot that's troubling about our country today, a lot of changes affecting us all. One of the big changes in America is that we're beginning to worry about each other. We are moving toward unselfish service to others, and the best way to adapt to change is to be part of it.

All of us, in our homes and our businesses, are challenged today to provide ways for relieving poverty and hunger in this country. We must find channels to help the illiterate and the underprivileged and the handicapped to become productive human beings, to give them the self-respect to go the rest of the way in independence. We are also challenged to preserve justice and freedom, not only in the law and the courts, but in our own hearts and minds.

"We should take nothing for granted.
Only an alert and knowledgeable citizenry
can compel the proper meshing of the huge
industrial and military machinery of defense
with our peaceful methods and goals so
that security and liberty may prosper together."
DWIGHT D. EISENHOWER, JANUARY 1961

WHAT CAN I DO?

Get involved. It is really as simple as that.

There are countless nationwide organizations that could use your time and support. And while they are national in scope, these organizations are entirely dependent on the individual citizen for any success they may have. Should you wish to have a more personal sense of involvement, somewhere in your own community there's a group or cause that needs you. Whatever time you can offer, whatever skill you possess, will be welcomed.

Speak your mind to your local officials, your Congressmen. Write a short, explicit letter; explain your stand. Your letter will be read. If you don't know your elected officials or where to write, ask your librarian or your League of Women Voters.

> *"Our proper business is improvement. Let our age be the age of improvement."*
> *DANIEL WEBSTER, FIRST BUNKER HILL MONUMENT ORATION*

THE AMERICA WE LOVE

Last Thanksgiving, *The New York Times* published a moving essay by a woman named Janina Atkins, who was a journalist in Poland until she came here in 1964. She told of feeling "something in the air in America which filled my soul with independence, and independence begot strength. Among some of our American-born friends it is not fashionable to be enthusiastic about America. But what we, the newcomers, see are not only the problems but all the democratic solutions being sought and applied. When I cast my vote for the first time as a free citizen of a free country, only then I realized what it means to have the power of participation in a democratic government...we are also in love with America...what luck and joy it is to live in a free country."

To love America is our right and privilege. To make it better is the responsibility of us all.

"We hold these Truths to be self-evident, that all Men are created equal, that they are endowed by their Creator with certain un-alienable Rights, that among these are Life, Liberty, and the Pursuit of Happiness."

DECLARATION OF INDEPENDENCE
JULY 4, 1776

INDEX

Labor Day, 36
Ladies' Home Journal, vii
Lasker, Mrs. Albert D.
League of Women Voters, 52
Lincoln, Abraham, 4, 5, 29, 39, 47
Lloyd, Harold, 40
Longfellow, Henry Wadsworth, 43

MacLeish, Archibald, 17
Maglie, Sal, 40
"Make America Better," vii, 11
Massasoit, Chief, 21
Mays, Willie, 40
Mecklinburg Day, 37
Moore, Marianne, 40
Mormons, 23-24
Moynihan, Daniel P., 45
Muir, John, 15
Muskie, Edmund, 32

Nash, Ogden, 46
National Association of Real Estate Boards, vii, 11
National Historic Preservation Act, 32
National Opinion Research Center, 33
National Park Service, 14
New Harmony, 6
New Republic, The, 39
New York Giants, 40
New York Times, The, 52
New York Yankees, 40
Nixon, Richard M., vi, 6, 39

Parke-Bernet Galleries, 28
Payne, John Howard, 28
Pickford, Mary, 40
Pioneer Day, 37
Polk, Patty, 5
Polynesian Cultural Center, 21-22, 32
Proverbs, 47
Psalms, 47

Raleigh, Sir Walter, 13
Real Estate Boards, see National Association of
Reese, Harold (Pee Wee), 40
Rizzuto, Phil, 40
Robinson, Jackie, 40
Roosevelt, Franklin D., 30
Ross, Betsy, 37

Sandburg, Carl, 21
Seward's Day, 37
Sierra Club, 15
Song of Solomon, 47
Standish, Miles, 5
Stanford, Leland, 29
Steinbeck, John, 1
Stendahl, Dr. Krister, 23
Stevenson, Adlai E., 7
Stork Club, 40
Swinburne, Algernon C., 44

Thanksgiving Day, 21, 37, 52
Thomson, Bobby, 40
Thoreau, Henry David, 6
Town Meeting Day, 37
T.R.B., 39
Truman, Harry S., 38
Twain, Mark, 29

"Uncle Sam," 38-39
United Nations, 38
Ute Indians, 21

Valentine's Day, 41
Vandiver, Willard Duncan, 25

Walden, 6
War of 1812, 38
Washington, George, 5, 37, 49
Webster, Daniel, 52
Whitman, Walt, 20
Whitney, Eli, 25
Wilson, Samuel, 38
World War II, 38

Young, Brigham, 24, 29

55